Stand-off in the Solent:
The American Civil War comes to Hamp
Michael Hughes

INTRODUCTION

The American Civil War was one of the most traumatic experiences in the history of the United States. Neither the Northern nor Southern states could have foreseen the scope or the horror of that conflict – considered to be the first modern war. At its end, in 1865, almost as many Americans had perished as in all of that country's other wars combined. Brothers opposed brothers; fathers and sons turned against one another – but from the horror of the conflict emerged a new Union, together with freedom and the promise of equality for African-American slaves.

For over 40 years Northerners and Southerners had argued with increasing vehemence over a number of issues. These included slavery, states rights, the conflict between a dynamic industrial North and a static agricultural South and the falling from political power of the South, which, since Thomas Jefferson's presidency at the turn of the century, had provided national leadership on seven occasions up to the 1850s. Whatever the causes of the war, it was the election of Abraham Lincoln as President of the United States in 1860 that shattered the fragile Union. Southerners were unwilling to live under a Republican administration dedicated to preventing the expansion of slavery into new territories. Consequently in December 1860, South Carolina seceded from the Union and in turn six other Southern states followed suit. A Confederate Government was established, initially at Montgomery, Alabama. (*See* p. 21 for a note on terms used in this Paper.) A few months later it was transferred to Richmond, Virginia, with Jefferson Davis its first, and as it turned out last, President. From the beginning the South insisted that all Federal (United States) fortifications be abandoned. However, the garrison at Fort Sumter in the harbour at Charleston, South Carolina, resisted until 12 April 1861. On that day Confederate guns opened fire on the fort and the Civil War began – a war that was to last almost exactly four years.

Within a few days of the fall of Fort Sumter, President Lincoln called for 75,000 volunteers to join the Union army. In the meantime the South made preparations to reinforce its State militia units with a large number of volunteers. In 1860 the British population in the North was nearly half a million, the result of large-scale unemployment at home and consequent emigration to the United States mainly in the 1840s and 1850s. Some of Hampshire's church vestry minutes provide a picture of emigration to North America in the 1830s, for example from parishes such as Wonston, Monk Sherborne and Hambledon (HRO COPY/555/17, 94M71/PO3, 49M69/PV1). Over 25% of British emigrants settled in New York State, with another 25% living in Pennsylvania, Ohio and Illinois. Unlike regiments founded for German and Irish emigrants, no English volunteer regiments were established, either in those states or any others. An attempt was made to raise one by English-born residents – the 36th New York Volunteer Regiment, but because in May 1861 the British Government adopted a stance of neutrality in the Civil War and following intercessions by the British Legation, the regiment was disbanded before it was officially enrolled into the Union army (Lonn 1951). Nevertheless over 50,000 Englishmen (excluding Welshmen, Scots and Irish) fought for the Union as soldiers and their blood was often spilt on the battlefields of the Civil War. Some were originally from Hampshire, like 21-year-old Corporal William Grant who was born in Portsmouth and served appropriately in the 11th New Hampshire Volunteer Regiment. He was subsequently captured by Confederate forces at the Battle of Cold Harbour, near Richmond, Virginia, in 1864. Another Hampshire soldier, John Orrill, was a private in the 6th New York Cavalry Regiment whilst William Berry, also born in 'Hampshire', became a captain in the 2nd New York Artillery Regiment. Unfortunately he was killed in one of the battles that raged around Petersburg in Virginia in 1864 (Ayling 1895; Phisterer 1912; National Archives, Record Group 94). Even Englishmen who had recently settled in the United States felt strongly about the future of their newly-adopted country. In 1863 a British-born carpenter, then a private in the 28th Massachusetts Regiment, rebuked his wife in Columbus, Ohio, and his father-in-law in England, for questioning his judgement in risking his life for Lincoln's war aims. He wrote: 'This is the first test of a modern free government in the act of sustaining itself against internal enemies. If it fail then the hopes of millions fall.' Later that year, in the Gettysburg campaign, he gave his life for those convictions. (McPherson 1994, 31-2.)

The possibility of an outbreak of civil war in the United States created concern in this country as reflected in newspaper editorials and questions asked in the House of Commons and the House of Lords. This concern was expressed in an editorial of the *Hampshire Chronicle*, published before news reached these shores of the fall of Fort Sumter:

> The latest American news is seriously changed in tone. We now learn that warlike rumours and the active naval operations of the government in Washington are creating intense excitement; and a very general impression prevailed that war would ensue immediately. (*HC* 20.4.1861.)

When news finally reached England of the outbreak of war, the editorial of the *Hampshire Chronicle* reported the comments of the *Daily News* that ' . . . the whole affair [is] utterly inexplicable – [to be] compared with cockneys fighting in London' (*HC* 27.4.1861).

'OPENING SHOTS': CHARLESTON AND THE WEST INDIES

One of Lincoln's first actions after the firing on Fort Sumter was to issue a proclamation concerning the blockade of the entire Confederacy's ports. The blockade would prevent both the export of cotton, upon which the South's fortunes relied, and the import of essential supplies, arms and munitions that their new armies would desperately need. The Confederacy did not have the industrial base to support a country at war; nor did the South have a large enough merchant fleet to bring in military supplies. For both ships and supplies, the South looked to England. Once the English realised the immense profits that could be made by running cargoes through the Northern blockade, by way of the West Indies, a large profitable trade opened up between the islands and the Confederacy. It was not only the South, however, that required arms and munitions for the war effort. The North also needed to be supplied with weapons and other essential war supplies and was, like the South, willing to purchase them from Britain or other western European nations. As well as carrying cargoes of Belgian, Austrian or French rifles, for example, both sides laid great store on having well-proven English Enfield rifle muskets for their infantry brigades and, in the case of the artillery regiments, English Whitworth cannon. The cavalry was also similarly supplied; the steamship *Saxonia* sailed from Southampton bound for a Northern port on 7 November 1861, carrying 7,000 carbines and 500 cavalry sabres (*OR*, ser. II, vol. 2, 1244).

However, both the new Confederacy and some of the European nations had doubts about the ability of the US Government to blockade effectively all the Southern ports and harbours. Also England and France declared their neutrality in May 1861, less than a month after the war had started. The Confederate states still hoped, however, that the stranglehold they had over the world's major supply of cotton would force both countries to break the blockade. Consequently in September 1861 the new Confederate Secretary of State, R. M. T. Hunter appointed James Mason, from Virginia, and John Slidell, from Louisiana, as Commissioners to Great Britain and France respectively (figs. 1-2). The Commissioners were sent to Europe to gain recognition for the Confederacy and thus persuade both nations to break the Northern blockade. They were also to act as purchasing agents for arms and materials.

To run the blockade out of Charleston, South Carolina, the Commissioners needed a fast vessel and one that would be able to bring back war munitions from England. As the Confederate Government, based in Richmond, Virginia, considered the envoys'

mission to be very important, the steamship *Nashville* was made available in late September for the voyage to Europe (fig. 3). The *Nashville*, a US mail steamer built in 1853, had arrived in Charleston in April, just before the capture of Fort Sumter. She was subsequently seized by the Confederacy to be fitted out as a privateer. The *Nashville*, a 1,200-ton side-

Fig. 3. The CSS *Nashville.*
US Navy Archives.

Fig. 4. Robert Pegram, captain of the *Nashville.*
Virginia Historical Society.

wheeler with a speed of 12 knots, faster than most ships on the Atlantic coast, had plied between Charleston and New York. She had also been chartered, on occasions, for the mail service between New York, Le Havre and Southampton. Speed and size made her a good choice as a blockade runner. Even as early as May, the Confederate Government wanted to arm the ship with 'as little publicity as possible', when she was being fitted out at Charleston. Her deck was found to be too weak to sustain the weight of heavy armaments, but nevertheless when she finally sailed in October she had been armed with two English Blakely rifled 12-pound guns. (*ORN*, ser. I, vol. 1, 94, 96; *ORN*, ser. I, vol. 6, 286-7; *ORN*, ser. II, vol. 1, 261, 334; *ST* 23.11.1861; Jones 1960, i, 233; Robertson 1928, 32-53; Wise 1988, 8-10.)

Lieutenant Robert Pegram was given command of the *Nashville* on 1 October 1861 and instructed to have her ready for a special mission as soon as possible. Pegram (fig. 4) was born at Dinwiddie Court House, Virginia, on 10 December 1811. At 17 he became a midshipman in the US Navy and then served in squadrons in the Mediterranean, Africa, Brazil, the Pacific and the East Indies. In 1841 he was promoted to Lieutenant and, while serving with the East India Squadron in 1855, led a detachment of

Fig. 5. Charleston, South Carolina, in early 1861. *Harper's Weekly.*

sailors to assist a British naval force to capture a flotilla of Chinese pirate ships. After Virginia joined the Confederacy in 1861 Pegram remained loyal to the state by resigning his commission with the US Navy. He then became a captain in the Virginia Navy, before being enrolled in the Confederate Navy. (*Virginia Cavalcade* 1965, 15, no. 2, 38-41; *Register of Officers of the Confederate States Navy 1861-1865* 1931; *ST* 23.11.1861; *Virginia Magazine of History and Biography* 1958, 66, 345-50.)

The *Nashville* was fitted out to take cabin passengers. They included the Commissioners and their staff, Mrs Slidell and family, and a Colonel J. L. Peyton. The Colonel was travelling on a special mission for the state of North Carolina and the Secretary of State for the Navy (*ORN*, ser. I, vol. 1, 96). The ship was also to carry several 'first-rate Carolinian and Georgian pilots' almost certainly to assist Confederate agents in England in sailing bought or appropriated supply ships or raiders returning to the South (*ORN*, ser. I, vol. 2, 94; *ORN*, ser. I, vol. 6, 286-7; *ORN*, ser. II, vol. 2, 94-6; *ST* 23.11.1861; Jones 1960, 233).

The Confederate ship is reported to have had a crew of 40, as well as her former captain and engineer on this 'special' mission. The crew included 26 foreigners, most of whom were English and Irish sailors (*ORN*, ser. I, vol. 2, 94; Lonn 1940, 297). Because of the urgent need for military supplies, Pegram was instructed to return from England with Enfield rifles, cannons, musket or rifle powder, flannel for artillery shells, lead and pig iron, as well as overcoats, black-leather waist belts, knapsacks, and bugles and swords. A sum of $100,000 for the cargo was to be made available to Pegram in England. This was to be achieved through the services of the recently appointed Confederate agent in Liverpool, James D. Bulloch, together with John Fraser and Company, Charleston's largest shipping firm who had offices in the same city (*ORN*, ser. II, vol. 2, 5; Jones 1960, 233). The company's Liverpool office traded under the name of Fraser, Trenholm and Company and became financial agents to the Confederate Government in England (Nepveux 1994, 7).

The departure of the Confederate Commissioners from Charleston, however, did not go according to plan (fig. 5). When news of their appointments and their missions to London and Paris reached Washington, the US Navy reacted by reinforcing the blockade of the Southern port. This meant that the only chance the *Nashville* had of leaving Charleston and eluding the blockading squadron was to negotiate the dangerous sandbars at the harbour entrance. Consequently an alternative strategy was adopted. The side-wheeler *Gordon*, the harbour patrol boat, faster and lighter and with a shallower

draft than the *Nashville*, was chartered by the Confederate Government. The boat would take the Commissioners as far as the West Indies, where they could take passage in a British mail ship bound for England (*ORN*, ser. I, vol. 1, 276-7).

The obvious value placed by the Confederacy on the mission to Europe is clearly demonstrated by the considerable cost of both purchasing, arming and fitting-out the *Nashville* and then of having to charter the *Gordon*, a fact not unnoticed by Commissioner Mason in a letter to his wife (Mason (ed.) 1906, 199). The presence in Richmond of Sir James Fergusson, a Conservative member of Parliament, may also have been significant. Having had a meeting with Confederate Secretary of State, R. M. T. Hunter, he may have also met the Commissioners shortly before their departure for Europe and discussed their forthcoming reception in London (PP GC/DE/71; *see also* Hughes 1999).

The *Gordon*, renamed the *Theodora* for the occasion, commanded by Captain Thomas Lockwood, finally left Charleston with the Commissioners on board in the early morning of 12 October, crossed the sandbar safely and passed through the blockading squadron without mishap. No doubt the decision to charter the *Gordon/Theodora* was also helped by the fact that a change of ship might deceive the US Navy into believing that the Commissioners were still to sail on the *Nashville* (*ORN*, ser. I, vol. 1, 114, 150). It has also been claimed that Southern newspapers, which laid a trail of false information concerning the departure of Mason and Slidell, aided this deception.

The deception appears to have worked. Having learned of the *Nashville*'s original mission, US Secretary of the Navy, Gideon Welles, assumed mistakenly that the Confederate Commissioners were to sail on her. He consequently requested Flag Officer Samuel Francis Du Pont, Commander of the

Fig. 6. Charles Adams, US Ambassador to England. *Harper's Weekly.*

South Atlantic Blockading Squadron, to send US warships after the Confederate ship, even though at that time she had not left her berth in Charleston. Du Pont was not happy with these instructions as he was planning an assault on Port Royal, South Carolina, in early November and he needed all the ships he could muster. Consequently only three ships were sent, including the USS *James Adger*, commanded by John B. Marchand. The *James Adger*, a three-masted side-wheeler (1,152 tons), was built in New York in 1851 and ran between New York and Charleston as a US mail steamer, operated by the same company that owned the *Nashville*. She was, however, luckier than the *Nashville* as she had left Charleston on 9 April, just before the surrender of Fort Sumter. She was then purchased by the US Government in July 1861 and converted into a warship. Commissioned at the Navy Yard on 20 September, she carried eight 32-pounder guns and one 20-pounder Parrott gun (*DANFS* 1968, iii, 488-9; *ORN*, ser. II, vol. 1, 112).

The other two ships sent by Du Pont were the USS *Connecticut* (Commander Woodhill) and the USS *Curlew* (Acting Commander Lieutenant Watmough). However, after some days at sea, and because of her limited range and size, the *Curlew* turned back to port while the *Connecticut* went as far as Bermuda. As neither of these two ships had received any information on the *Nashville*'s whereabouts, the *Connecticut* returned to the United States coast on 24 October (*ORN*, ser. I, vol. 1, 113-18), leaving the *James Adger* to continue the search for the elusive Confederate ship.

In the meantime, the Confederate Commissioners on board the *Theodora* had arrived in Providence, Nassau, in the Bahamas, on 14 October. Since their arrival was too late for the local ship to St Thomas in the Virgin Islands, the sailing point for British ships bound for England and Europe, the envoys proceeded on to Cardenas in Cuba and from there overland to Havana, arriving on 22 October. Because it was concerned about possible Federal intervention, the Confederate Government felt that the Commissioners might be safer on the British West Indies mail ship *Trent* that was soon to sail for St Thomas. Once in St Thomas, the Commissioners could then transfer to another mail ship, the *La Plata*, a wooden-hulled paddle steamer that would soon sail to England. However, the local Federal 'intelligence' learned of the arrival of the Commissioners in Havana and on 8 November the US warship *San Jacinto* 'removed' Mason and Slidell and their secretaries from the *Trent*, an action which drew protests from the British and subsequently developed into the so-called 'Trent Affair'. (For an account of the *Trent* Affair *see*, for example: Adams 1925; Crook 1974; Fairfax n.d.; Ferris 1977; Musicant

1995. A full account is also given in *OR* and *ORN*.) In the meantime John Slidell's family and other passengers were allowed to proceed on to St Thomas where they boarded the *La Plata* bound for Southampton (*ORN*, ser. I, vol. 1, 150).

THE *JAMES ADGER* AT SOUTHAMPTON

During this drama, Commander Marchand of the *James Adger* was continuing his search of the north Atlantic for the *Nashville*, which unknown to him was still stuck in Charleston. He eventually reached the Irish coast on 30 October, having survived heavy weather in the Atlantic which caused damage to his ship. He subsequently docked at Queenstown in southern Ireland, for repairs and for supplies of coal. The ship then continued its fruitless search for the *Nashville*, but once again bad weather, this time in the English Channel, forced her to put into Falmouth in Cornwall for further coal supplies. The need for additional structural repairs and more coal finally forced the *James Adger* into Southampton in the first week of November (*ORN*, ser. I, vol. 1, 125-6, 129, 156).

The arrival of the Federal warship was immediately reported by the *Southampton Times*:

> A Federal warship arrived on Wednesday 7th. English shipping agents, Messrs J. Wolf and Company were employed to coal the ship and to repair some damage which she had sustained during the voyage from New York. (*ST* 9.11.1861.)

Once in Southampton (incorrectly identified as London in Crook 1974, 121), Captain Marchand reported to the US Ambassador, Charles Adams (fig. 6). Marchand felt that once he had refuelled and undergone necessary repairs, there was no reason why he should not return to the United States as his instructions were to intercept the Confederate warship carrying Mason and Slidell, and 'not to interfere with any other ship sailing under a foreign flag' (ORN, ser. I, vol. 1, 128-9, 156).

Even before the news of the capture of the Confederate Commissioners reached London, the British Government had become very agitated over the arrival of the James Adger, especially as many politicians favoured the South. Consequently, the Prime Minister, Lord Palmerston asked the American Ambassador for an explanation. He received an assurance that it was only the Nashville that Captain Marchand had been ordered to capture and that he was ordered not to interfere with any other foreign shipping. Nevertheless HMS Phaeton, a Royal Naval frigate from Portsmouth, was ordered to take station off Yarmouth on the Isle of Wight, to watch the James Adger's movements. Adams was obviously concerned, and probably embarrassed, at the presence of the James Adger. He also stated to Palmerston that he had already instructed Marchand to return to the United States (ORN, ser. I, vol. 1, 160-1; Adams 1925, i, 206-11; Crook 1974, 126). Palmerston was probably not completely convinced by Adams's assurances and saw the whole episode and the presence of a US warship in British waters as part of an unfriendly plot by the North.

It would appear that Marchand's instructions were changed after he had left Southampton, for he was ordered to keep a look out and capture merchant ships sailing from England to Confederate ports carrying munitions. Accordingly, he informed US Navy Secretary Welles that he would on his return journey try and trace the whereabouts of the Gladiator, an English ship chartered by the Confederacy that had recently left London bound for Bermuda or Nassau, carrying, amongst other war supplies, Enfield rifles and Whitworth cannon. However, the James Adger had no luck in her search for ships carrying contraband of war and arrived back in the United States on 2 December 1861. (ORN, ser. I, vol. 1, 160-1, 202, 226-7.)

THE VOYAGE OF THE NASHVILLE

While the activities of the James Adger were in the spotlight on both sides of the Atlantic, the Confederate Secretary of the Navy, Stephen Mallory, had made plans to send the Nashville to England in order to bring back precious war supplies needed by the Confederate armies. The Nashville still carried Mason and Slidell's letters of introduction to the British and French governments, as well as Colonel Peyton (ORN, ser. II, vol. 1, 633). However, bad

weather and the Nashville's inability to clear the sandbars at the entrance to the harbour, meant that time was of the essence. Mallory, therefore, frustrated with the delays, demanded that Pegram make ready to sail. Once the weather improved, Pegram removed sufficient coal to lighten the ship so that she could just clear the tops of the sandbars, and on the night of 26 October Nashville slipped anchor and left bound for England. She scraped the sandbar as she passed over it, but Pegram successfully ran the Federal blockade which by now consisted of the USS Susquehanna and USS Monticello and possibly two other warships (ORN, ser. I, vol. 6, 359-63; Pegram).

The Nashville then quietly and uneventfully made her way across the Atlantic. As Pegram had had to leave Charleston with insufficient coal supplies to get him to England, he had to re-coal at Bermuda. He arrived at the island on 30 October. However, the Royal Naval officers stationed on Bermuda refused to provision the Confederate ship. The reason given for the refusal was that a large English and French fleet, bound for Mexico, was expected in a few weeks and they had priority over available coal supplies. Consequently Pegram was forced to sail to the adjacent island of St George where coal was made available from a civilian source. On 3 November Pegram met up with the senior Confederate agent in England, Captain James Bulloch, who was on his way to report to Mallory and the Confederate Government in Richmond. (On the coaling of ships in the West Indies during the Civil War see also Blume 1995, 116-41.) Having re-coaled, the Nashville finally left St George on 5 November and headed for Southampton (Pegram; ORN, ser. I, vol. 1, 745). Stephen Wise incorrectly states in his book that the Nashville reached Liverpool, rather than Southampton, in November 1861, where it was hoped to renovate her as a warship (Wise 1988, 61). He may have been confused by a published but incorrect communication between the US Consul at Bermuda and the US Navy Yard in New York, which stated 'the Nashville is lightly armed and carries large amounts of treasure and bound for Liverpool' (ORN, ser. I, vol. 1, 219).

The ship was buffeted by storms during her voyage across the Atlantic which necessitated frequently shifting the coal load from the front of the ship to the stern and back again in order to maintain stability. The bad weather also caused some damage to her upper deck structures and paddle housing which required urgent repairs (Pegram). However, on the morning of 19 November, 40 miles off the north-west French coast in the English Channel, the Nashville attacked and captured the US Harvey Birch (fig. 7). The Harvey Birch was a merchantman on her way to New York from the French port of Le Havre, where she had landed wheat and taken on ballast

Fig. 7. 'The CSS *Nashville* Burning the *Harvey Birch*', oil painting by Duncan McFarlane, 1864.
Peabody Museum, Salem, Massachusetts.

Fig. 8. The Sailor's Home, Canute Road, Southampton, a print dating from the mid nineteenth century.
Hampshire Record Office, TOP286/2/392(L).

(*HA* 23.11.1861; *ORN*, ser. I, vol. 1, 156) When captured, the 1,600-ton ship, built in 1854 at Mystic, Connecticut, had a crew of 23 and three officers, including Captain M. Nelson (*ST* 23.11.1861). As a consequence of her action, the *Nashville* became the first warship to fly the Confederate colours in British waters. She was also the first Confederate warship to capture a US ship in European waters.

Pegram ordered Captain Nelson to ensure that his crew collected all their belongings before they boarded the *Nashville*. Then, once on board, the crew of the *Harvey Birch*, with the exception of the officers, were clapped in irons, although they were well treated during the voyage to Southampton. The merchantman was then cleared of all her charts, provisions and live stock and set on fire. It was later stated by Captain Nelson that during the *Nashville*'s voyage to Southampton, the Confederate captain attempted, without success, to persuade Nelson and his crew to take the oath of allegiance and swear not to take up arms against the South (*ORN*, ser. I, vol. 1, 746).

THE *NASHVILLE* AT SOUTHAMPTON

On 20 November the *Nashville* sailed across the English Channel and took on a Southampton pilot off the Isle of Wight. The following morning she anchored in Southampton Water, off the mouth of the River Itchen (fig. 9). Later that same day she took up a berth in the Outer Tidal Basin at Southampton Docks and landed all the officers and crew of the *Harvey Birch* (Pegram). Captain Nelson went first to Captain Britten, the US Consul in the town, to make

7

Fig. 9. Detail from a 'new complete and correct map of
Southampton and its suburban district' by Philip Brannon,
mid-nineteenth century.
Hampshire Record Office, TOP286/2/341(L).

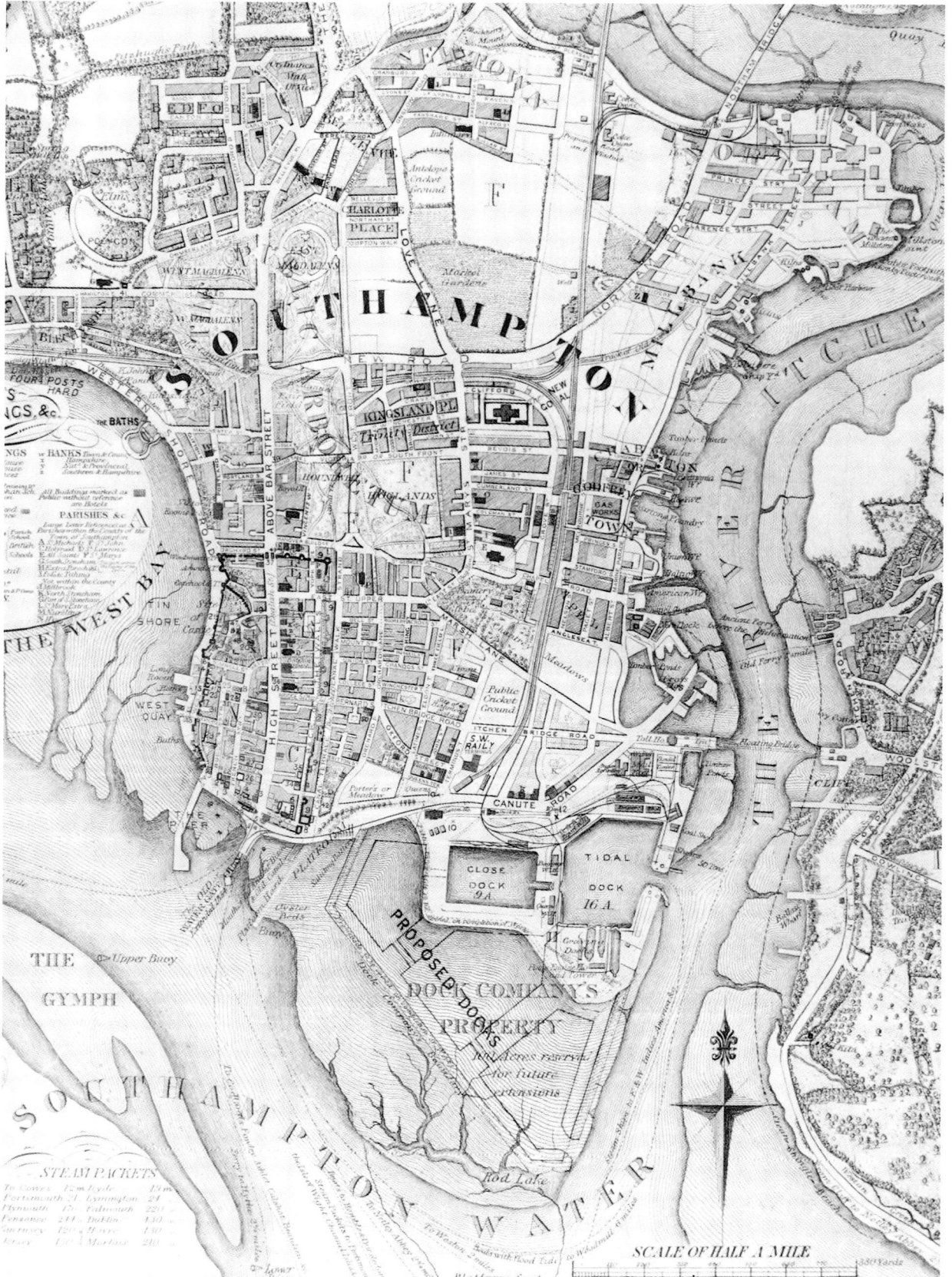

arrangements for his crew to be given temporary lodgings at the Sailor's Home in Canute Road, a charitable institution for sailors on shore leave (fig. 8). A few days later they were put on board a passenger-carrying ship, the *Hansa*, which was sailing to New York. Later Nelson accompanied the US Consul to London to inform the American Ambassador Adams of the events of the past few days (*ST* 30.11.1861).

The arrival of the Confederate warship caused a great deal of public excitement in Southampton and elsewhere in Hampshire. Crowds gathered at the quayside to watch the docking and would have clambered on board had a notice not been placed at the foot of the gangway forbidding admittance except on official business. However, the Mayor of Southampton, Councillor F. Perkins, was among the ship's visitors that day as well as Captain Charles Patey, the senior Royal Naval officer in the town (*ST* 23.11.1861, 30.11.1861). As well as being the Admiralty's representative in Southampton, he was also Superintendent of the Packet Service and an Additional Captain on HMS *Victory* (*HA* 23.11.1861; *Navy List* 1862, ii, 159-224). Once the *Nashville* had docked, Colonel Peyton left for London carrying a letter of introduction from Pegram to one of the Confederate agents in the city, William L. Yancey. Colonel Peyton appraised Yancey of the events of the past few days and of Navy Secretary Mallory's instructions, which almost certainly concerned the purchase of war supplies (Pegram).

A week later Captain Nelson, accompanied by a Mr Pearcey, who represented a firm of London solicitors acting on his behalf, made an application to the Southampton Magistrates for a search warrant with a view to recovering his chronometer and barometer and the *Harvey Birch*'s papers from the *Nashville*. Nelson had preceded the application with one to the Lord Mayor of London, who had decided it was better dealt with by a local magistrate. The Lord Mayor did, however, inform Captain Nelson that had the *Nashville* been lying in London Docks he would have granted the application! Unfortunately the Southampton court took a different view and refused the application on the grounds that an opponent had a right to take anything he chose under such circumstances as existed in this particular case. This decision was upheld by the British High Court (*HA* 30.11.1861).

News of the *Nashville*'s arrival with her prisoners had also been telegraphed to the Admiralty and the British Government. Consequently, within a few days some English national newspapers were condemning the loss of the *Harvey Birch*. The ship's destruction they claimed was an affront to Her Majesty's Government and its neutrality in the Civil War. Some papers, especially the *Morning Star*, were vitriolic

concerning the *Nashville* and her captain, whilst a more moderate but nevertheless critical comment was made in *The Times*.

> The Southerns will, perhaps, ask us what right we have to allow the *James Adger* to refit; the Northerns will, perhaps, protest if we allow the *Nashville* to refit. We probably should have been in our strict right if we had refused to have anything to do with either of these ships. We shall wait with some impatience to have the law of nations, so far as it rules, for these inconvenient visitors, expounded to us. It would be clearly to our interest to keep them both out of our harbours. If, however, we cannot do this, we suppose we must let them both in alike, under pain of forfeiture of the Royal word. (*The Times* 22.11.1861.)

On the question of neutrality, the British Government had in May 1861 already issued a proclamation which recognised the belligerency, but not the independence, of the Confederacy, an action which not surprisingly earned the hostility of the North (Bourne 1970, 90). British neutrality laws, however, permitted the *Nashville* (and the *James Adger*) to enter British ports for the purpose of provisioning, even though they were ships of war commissioned by belligerent powers. Although armed ships or privateers from either side were forbidden from carrying prizes of war into British ports, the *Nashville* had not violated this rule as she had burnt the *Harvey Birch* at sea and immediately on arrival had released her crew (Crook 1974, 118).

Whatever the rights or wrongs of the British Government's position, the capture and burning of the *Harvey Birch* was considered an act of piracy by the American Northern press. Anti-British feelings were inflamed in the Northern states, especially as the *Nashville* was being repaired and refuelled by the British in a British port. The situation was not helped when the Lincoln administration refused to concede belligerent rights to the Confederacy. Consequently, the *Nashville*'s status remained uncertain, even though she was, as far as the British were concerned, a warship permitted by neutrality laws to enter British ports for provisioning and necessary repairs. In fact the view of the British Government was that the *Nashville* was only enjoying the same 'hospitality' which had been accorded the Northern warship *James Adger* when she had docked at Southampton.

Although overshadowed by the *Trent* Affair, the news of which was about to reach England, these events brought the war uncomfortably close to English shores, and could themselves have caused a major international incident. As William Seaward, Lincoln's Secretary of State, commented towards the end of 1861: 'There were also other currents [as distinct from the *Trent* Affair] that seemed to be

Fig. 10. The CSS *Nashville* at Southampton.
Harper's Weekly.

bringing the two countries in collision.' (Ferris 1976, 197.) There is even the possibility that knowledge of the Commissioners' visits to London and Paris was deliberately leaked by the Confederacy in order to create antagonism between England and the Union (*see also* Perkins 1993, i, 217). The Confederate Government, although guarded in its comments, in private would have almost certainly welcomed the wave of anti-British emotion and rhetoric in the North, and the consequent anti-Union public opinion in England. They must have felt that support for the Southern cause was gaining ground, even within British Government circles. One member of Parliament, for example, declared that if this insult (the removal of the Commissioners on their lawful way to Britain from a British ship which had raised the British flag upon meeting the *San Jacinto*) were not atoned, he saw no use for the flag and that he would recommend 'the British colours be torn into shreds and sent to Washington for the use of the Presidential water-closets' (*OR* ser. II, vol. 2, 1107).

Eventually, in late November, the mail ship *La Plata* reached the Isle of Wight and was met by Lieutenant Pegram, who had come by steam tug from Southampton to meet the Confederate Commissioners. Once on board the mail ship he learnt for the first time, as did the British Government later that day, of Captain Wilkes's removal of Mason and Slidell from the *Trent* on 8 November. Pegram

then took Mrs Slidell and her family, who had been travelling on the *La Plata*, back to the *Nashville* where, after having entertained them, he saw them safely on a train to London (*HA* 30.11.1861).

The British Government kept a close watch on the *Nashville*'s repairs in Southampton Docks to prevent war supplies destined for Confederate troops being loaded on board (fig. 10). Nothing was allowed to be done excepting what was absolutely necessary to make her seaworthy. Although Pegram had requested improvements to his armaments, he was not permitted by the British authorities to procure additional arms or ammunition (*ORN*, ser. I, vol. 1, 745-9; *ORN*, ser. II, vol. 2, 118). For example, the local shipwright who was employed to undertake some of the repairs was not even allowed to use some specially prepared pieces of oak to strengthen the decks for gun mountings. As a consequence the timber still lay on the quayside when the *Nashville* finally left port, with empty cargo holds, in February 1862. On 5 December the *Nashville* was moved into the dry dock and from then until 30 December, including Christmas Day, a large number of 'carpenters, caulkers and mechanics' worked on her. After leaving dry dock she returned to her former berth and began taking on coal during the first few days of January 1862 (Pegram).

Because of the delay caused by the American Government refusing to release the Confederate Commissioners immediately or to offer apologies to the British, in late 1861 and early 1862 British troop reinforcements were sent to Canada. In late December 1861, for example, a battalion of the Guards regiment sailed in two ships from Southampton watched by officers of the *Nashville*

Fig. 12. The USS *Tuscarora*.
US Navy Archives.

(*ILN* 28.12.1861; fig. 11). It was also during this period that some of the *Nashville*'s crew deserted the ship, probably having made use of the voyage to return home. One was caught and court-martialled (*ORN*, ser. I, vol. 1, 746). By the end of the first week of January 1862, Pegram was ready to leave Southampton, but delayed his departure, perhaps to await news of the Confederate Commissioners who had recently been released by the Federal authorities. On 9 January 1862, Thomas Stopher, the Winchester architect, recorded in his diary:

> News arrived today of the peaceful settlement of the American Question by the Americans giving up Messrs Mason and Slidell and apologising for the affront (HRO 21M85W/1.)

'NORTH VERSUS SOUTH': THE USS *TUSCARORA* ARRIVES

On hearing of the capture and destruction of the *Harvey Birch* by the *Nashville*, US Navy Secretary Gideon Welles had ordered the Federal warship USS *Tuscarora* to sail to England in order to shadow and destroy the Confederate ship (fig. 12). The USS *Tuscarora* was a new screw corvette, constructed at the Philadelphia Navy yards in June 1861. She was armed with nine heavy guns, including two pivoted eleven-inch Dahlgrens, six broadside guns and a rifled-Parrott gun on the forecastle (*DANFS* 1981, vii, 362-4), and was commanded by Captain Craven. Craven later commanded the USS *Brooklyn* during the Mississippi River campaign in 1862 and was drowned in August 1864 when the USS *Tecumseh*

sank beneath him in the Battle for Mobile Bay (Sifakis 1988, i, 92). The *Tuscarora*'s sister ship was the USS *Kearsage*, which finally sank the famous Confederate blockade runner the CSS *Alabama*.

The *Tuscarora* left New York on 15 December 1861, a few days after she had been commissioned, with instructions to proceed at once to the English Channel and ascertain the whereabouts of the *Nashville*. Craven's prime objective was to seize the Confederate ship without infringing the neutral rights of the British Government. He was also made aware by Welles that several ships, including the *Bermuda*, the *Gladiator* and the *Fingal* had been armed and fitted out for the Confederate Government in British ports. Craven was ordered to stop them, if possible, on their way from the West Indies to Confederate ports (*ORN*, ser. I, vol. 1, 230-1) but he apparently did not encounter any of them, and, after a rough passage across the Atlantic, he stopped at Fayal in the Canary Islands for coal supplies. The *Tuscarora* finally arrived in Southampton Water on the afternoon of 8 January 1862, the day on which the British received a telegraphed message that Mason and Slidell had been released by the Federal Government (*ANG* 11.1.1862; *ORN*, ser. I, vol. 1, 275; Crook 1974, 162).

With her superior armaments, the *Tuscarora* was a formidable opponent for the *Nashville*, which would not have stood a chance against the firepower of the Federal ship in a one-to-one contest. The only advantage that the *Nashville* had over the *Tuscarora* was her speed. The 'cat and mouse game' between a

Fig. 13. Lithograph showing Southampton Docks in the 1860s.
Southampton City Heritage Services.

blockade runner, the *Nashville*, and a blockader, the *Tuscarora*, a game so often played out along the Carolina coastline, had now transferred from Charleston to Southampton – the Civil War had arrived in England!

On her arrival in Southampton Water, the *Tuscarora* moored off the mouth of the River Itchen, water through which the *Nashville* would have to sail to make her escape. As soon as he had moored the ship, Captain Craven sought permission from the captain of HMS *Dauntless*, moored in Southampton Water, to fire a 21-gun salute in memory of Prince Albert. (Queen Victoria's husband had died on 13 December, on the anniversary of the death of George Washington 62 years earlier.) However, as the Queen had expressed the wish that no guns be fired in the vicinity of Osborne House, on the Isle of Wight, the salute did not take place (*ST* 18.1.1862).

According to the Southampton and Hampshire newspapers, the arrival of another Federal warship created a further great flurry of interest, both locally and in other parts of the country. Thomas Stopher again commented in his diary:

> A great deal of excitement at Southampton just now as there is a Confederate steamer the *Nashville* in the docks and the *Tuscarora* a United

States frigate is now lying in the river watching her. (HRO 21M85W/1, 15.1.1862.)

Two days after his arrival, Captain Craven announced that he would put to sea as soon as the *Nashville* left Southampton and then pursue her into the English Channel. He therefore attempted to keep a close watch on the *Nashville*'s activities, to make sure that he was warned of her impending departure. However, Philip Hedge, the Docks Superintendent, discovered three armed men and an officer from the *Tuscarora* in the docks one night, watching the Confederate warship; they had been carrying dark lanterns and signalling equipment. A few days later Craven tried again to observe the *Nashville* closely, this time from a hired pilot boat, but once again he was foiled, on this occasion by the Royal Navy. (*ANG* 11.1.1862; *ORN*, ser. I, vol. 1, 277-8, 751; *ST* 18.1.1862; fig. 13.) Ambassador Adams then requested Craven to exercise caution whilst at Southampton and not to land any more men and risk a confrontation with the British authorities. Adams also informed Craven of the presence of a British ship, the *Pacific*, at Southampton. According to his sources, the ship had recently been purchased by the Confederacy and when fitted out was to be sailed to Nassau (*ORN*, ser. I, vol. 1, 276-8; *ST* 23.1.1862).

In the meantime, Craven had also requested the presence of another Federal warship so that both outlets to the docks at Southampton could be guarded (*ORN*, ser. I, vol. 1, 277-8). However, Her Majesty's Government was highly sensitive to what was happening, especially after Lord Russell (fig. 14), the Foreign Secretary, had learnt from Ambassador Adams of Craven's request. Adams had also requested further US warships to patrol the English Channel in order to protect US merchant shipping at Liverpool and Le Havre, afraid to sail because of the presence in north-western European waters of Confederate raiders (PP GC/RU/693-9). However, no additional warships were forthcoming, either to Craven's aid, or to guard US merchant ships. This was probably because all available Federal warships either were tied up with the blockade of Confederate ports and harbours or were involved in joint land and sea expeditions to capture strategic coastal positions in North Carolina.

Because of the diplomatic problems created by the presence and actions of the three American warships in English waters between the end of 1861 and the first two months of 1862, the British Government began to enforce the rules that appertained to belligerent sea-going vessels. Warships and raiders from both sides in the Civil War were prohibited from using English home or colonial ports, except for provisioning and repairs. Whilst originally there was no limit to the time such ships could spend provisioning or having repairs carried out, in early 1862 the Government enforced a time limit of 24 hours on Federal and Confederate ships alike, which meant that such ships were required to leave a British port within 24 hours of their arrival. However, the Government was prepared to allow exceptions to the 24-hour rule: first, if the need to shelter due to bad weather at sea could be demonstrated; secondly, if there was a need for urgent repairs to make the ship in question sufficiently seaworthy to proceed on her voyage; and thirdly, where necessary provisions for the crew were urgently required. The 24-hour rule could also be extended if a stronger ship blockaded a weaker one (in terms of armaments), especially if the tactics as later employed by the *Tuscarora* at Southampton were used. The coaling of warships or raiders was also limited in that only enough coal could be loaded to enable them to reach the nearest home port (*ANG* 1.2.1862; *see also* Blume 1995, 116-41).

Because of the situation at Southampton, Lord Russell gave instructions that if one of the belligerent ships left Southampton, the other was not to follow for 24 hours (PP GC/RU/693). As a result of the Government's decision, Captain Patey, the senior Royal Naval officer in Southampton, came on board HMS *Dauntless*, which was anchored in Southampton Water, almost certainly to inform the captain of the Government's concern and the need to keep a watchful eye on the two American ships. An additional 150 seamen and a party of Royal Marine artillerymen later complemented the crew of HMS *Dauntless* (engaged on coastguard service at the time and commanded by Captain Heath). Anchored close by was HMS *Argus*, a despatch boat commanded by Captain Wincroft, which had been sent from Portsmouth. Sailors from both *Dauntless* and *Argus* were also posted on guard in the docks to prevent any hostile confrontation from either ship (PRO ADM 53, 7900; *HA* 18.1.1862). As if this was not enough British military might, HMS *Shannon*, a screw frigate of the Channel Squadron commanded by Captain O. J. Jones (PRO ADM 53, 8189), also from Portsmouth, stood by at Spithead to assist in any awkward situation that might arise between the *Tuscarora* and the *Nashville*. A contingent of Marine artillerymen was also posted to Hurst Castle, whilst a chain of telegraphic communication was established between HMS *Victory* (also the flagship of the Commander-in-Chief, at Portsmouth), HMS *Shannon* and HMS *Warrior*, the latter two stationed off Portsmouth, and HMS *Dauntless* in Southampton Water (PRO ADM 53, 7900 and 8189; *Navy List* 1862, ii, 159-224; fig. 15).

On 11 January, the day the Government issued their instructions regarding the two American ships at Southampton, both Craven and Pegram received an official notification from Captain Patey of the Government's determination to enforce the 24-hour

Fig. 15. Detail from a mid nineteenth-century map of Hampshire and the Isle of Wight, showing Southampton Water and the Solent, with the Needles and Hurst Castle in the west, and Spithead and Portsmouth in the east. *Hampshire Record Office, 139M89/1/15.*

rule that if either ship left port the other could not follow for 24 hours. Patey had also received orders that, if necessary, he was to detain one vessel until the other had had 24 hours' start. (*ORN* ser. I, vol. 1, 279, 749-51.)

During these events, the two ships needed provisioning and the task was given to two Southampton brothers. J. H. Cooksey took care of the *Nashville*, whilst George Cooksey provisioned the *Tuscarora*. Whilst none of the crew of the *Tuscarora* was allowed on shore, and officers were only allowed to pick up provisions, officers from the *Nashville* were seen on a number of occasions enjoying the ambience of the town centre. The confinement of the Federal warship's crew may have been caused by a smallpox outbreak that was reported to have been on board (*HC* 11.1.1862).

Craven is reported to have been very unhappy with 'British cussedness and officialdom' over the 24-hour rule and in the light of Craven's concerns, Charles Adams, the American Ambassador, requested an explanation from the British Government of Captain Patey's demands. In the meantime he reiterated to Craven that he was not to put himself and his ship in conflict with the port authorities, however disagreeable that might be.

Craven also sent a message to Gideon Welles, claiming that 'not only is he not permitted to remain in port for more than 24 hours, but is prohibited from taking on coal more than once in three months thus depriving him of being able to cruise the English coast' (*ORN* ser. I, vol. 1, 295, 299).

The events that took place from 11 January until the end of the month do tend, however, to suggest that Craven fully intended to try and break the 24-hour rule. He would notify the port authorities 24 hours in advance that he would be leaving his mooring, and then sail out to sea, turn around and return later in the day to Southampton. On his return he would immediately notify the port authorities once more of his intention to depart again, 24 hours later. It is probable that Craven thought that the ship giving first notice of departure would have priority and thus the advantage over his opponent. Evidence exists that Craven actually carried out his bluff on three separate occasions – 13, 15 and 20 January 1862 (PRO ADM 53, 7900).

Captain Patey must have been aware of Craven's attempts at deception. Nevertheless, for reasons hard to understand, on 27 January he informed both Pegram and Craven that the *Tuscarora* should leave Southampton on the following day and that Pegram

would have to wait for 24 hours before the *Nashville* could leave its berth (*ORN*, ser. I, vol. 1, 294-5; Pegram). Naturally, Pegram was not particularly happy with Patey's instructions, which he saw as placing him and his ship at a disadvantage. Consequently he appealed to the First Lord of the Admiralty, Edward Seymour, 12th Duke of Somerset. In his letter to the First Lord on 27 January, Pegram stressed the 'inevitable capture' of the *Nashville* if the US warship was allowed to leave first. He also stated his belief that there had been 'some strange misconception' and enclosed a copy of Patey's orders. Pegram then wrote that he had paid 'the strictest regard to that neutrality which has been so solemnly proclaimed by Her Majesty's Government' and appealed for reconsideration of his instructions (Pegram). His appeal to the First Lord may also have been written in the knowledge that the press had recently referred to Pegram's pre-war exploits in China, which the British military had admired at the time.

The Confederate Commissioners finally arrived at Southampton from the West Indies on 29 January. Although Slidell went almost immediately to London, Mason remained until evening in the Radley Hotel, Southampton, where officers of the *Nashville* visited him. On reaching London later, Mason immediately communicated with the Secretary of State, R. M. T. Hunter, regarding the attitude of the British Government towards the *Nashville* in Southampton (*ORN*, ser. I, vol. 1, 751). He was also called on by Sir James Fergusson, who had met Hunter in Richmond the previous year, to congratulate him on his release by the Federal Government and on his safe arrival in London (*OR*, ser. II, vol. 2, 1242; Hughes 1999).

Fig. 17. Print entitled 'The Rival American Warships and the English Guardship at Southampton' taken from the *Penny Illustrated Paper*, 15 February 1862. USS *Tuscarora* is on the left, HMS *Shannon* in the centre and CSS *Nashville* on the right.
Hampshire Record Office, TOP286/2/392(L).

THE RIVAL AMERICAN WAR-SHIPS AND THE ENGLISH GUARD-SHIP AT SOUTHAMPTON.—see page 108

In the meantime at Southampton, Craven gave notice that he would follow Patey's orders but leave Southampton at 11.00 a.m. on Tuesday 29 January. However, when Tuesday morning arrived, Craven claimed that because of the bad weather he would have to delay his departure until Wednesday. Captain Patey, on the other hand, did not consider the weather a sufficient reason for delaying departure any longer so he expressly requested that Craven should leave immediately (*ORN*, ser. I, vol. 1, 295). The *Tuscarora* then left her moorings at the mouth of the Itchen, sailed down Southampton Water and anchored off Yarmouth, on the Isle of Wight, before sailing back again to her former position in Southampton Water later in the

day (fig. 16). Once again Craven was up to his by now familiar tricks. Two days later, on 31 January, once again having given 24 hours' notice, the *Tuscarora* left her moorings and sailed to a position off Yarmouth, where this time she remained for four days (PRO ADM 53, 8189). Whilst there she received signals from Southampton, via Hurst Castle, concerning the movements of the *Nashville*. On 3 February Craven sailed out past the Needles and down to Portland, on the Dorset coast, before suddenly changing course and heading back towards the Solent where he moored off Cowes. The reason behind this move was, according to Craven, because he needed coal and had to settle accounts for his provisioning at Southampton. However, his motive

16

no doubt was to try and fool the authorities and capture the *Nashville* as she left the next day (*ST* 8.2.1862).

In fact, this was an ill-judged move by Craven as it gave the *Nashville* the chance she had been waiting for. If Pegram now gave notice that he was leaving, the *Tuscarora* would have to wait, under the watchful eyes of the British Navy off the Isle of Wight, for 24 hours before she could follow the Confederate ship. Consequently, Lieutenant Pegram, having learnt of the *Tuscarora*'s movements, immediately gave 24 hours' notice that he would leave port the following day, 4 February. On being made aware of this, Captain Patey went immediately to Cowes in a steam launch and gave notice to Captain Craven that he could not leave within 24 hours of the departure of the Confederate ship. He also gave orders for HMS *Shannon* who was in the vicinity, to be prepared to enforce the 24-hour rule if necessary (*ST* 8.2.1862).

The *Nashville* had cleared the docks by 4 p.m. on 4 February, under the capable hands of Mr Bowyer, a Southampton pilot, who took her past Cowes (and a mortified Captain Craven) into the English Channel. As the Confederate ship passed down the Solent, HMS *Shannon* shifted her position to bar the *Tuscarora*'s way. The Federal warship was held until the following day, by which time the *Nashville* was some 200 miles away (fig. 17).

Mr Bowyer, the pilot, reported afterwards that before he left the Confederate ship, he had been asked by the officers to give their compliments to the officers of the *Tuscarora*, whom he might see before they left, 24 hours later. He was also requested to inform the same officers that if the Federal ship could make $16^1/2$ knots, it might be able to catch the *Nashville*. According to the *Nashville*'s engineer, he had so arranged the engine valves that if captured she could be blown up at a moment's notice and 'that if the people in Southampton heard of the capture of the *Nashville*, they should also have heard an explosion' (*ST* 8.2.1862).

THE END OF THE *NASHVILLE*

Having left Southampton and escaped the Federal warship, the *Nashville* started her return voyage to the Southern States. On reaching Bermuda on 20 February, she re-coaled. Whilst there, Pegram received unexpected assistance from the master of the Confederate schooner *Pearl*, which had run aground on the island's coastline. The master offered to pilot the *Nashville* into Beaufort, North Carolina. Pegram was returning home with empty cargo holds – not having been able to obtain the war supplies in England he had been asked to bring back by Mallory. But as if to make amends, after leaving Bermuda, the *Nashville* captured the US schooner

Robert Gifillan (Captain Smith) which was on a voyage from Philadelphia to Haiti. After its cargo and crew had been removed the US ship was set on fire, a repeat of the *Harvey Birch* affair (*ORN*, ser. I, vol. 1, 747-8).

At the end of February the *Nashville* arrived off Beaufort. But having seen US warships, including the USS *State of Georgia*, blockading the harbour entrance, Pegram bluffed his way through by raising the Union 'Stars and Stripes' (fig. 18). Eventually the *Nashville* arrived in safe waters at Morehead City, near Beaufort, on 28 February. At the end of his report to the Confederate Government, Lieutenant Pegram praised certain members of his crew, including Frank Dawson, a young Englishman. Dawson, who had served as an ordinary seaman, had apparently left family, home and friends in England in order to fight for the Confederate cause. Subsequently Pegram gave him a position as his personal clerk (Pegram's report appears in *ORN*, ser. I, vol. 1, 745-9). After his time on the *Nashville*, Pegram spent the next two years of the war in Richmond, Virginia, assisting in the building of, and eventually commanding, the CSS *Richmond* and her sister ship the CSS *Virginia II*. In 1864 he returned to England once more, this time to assist in the purchase and fitting out of ships for the Confederacy. However, he only managed to secure one ship before the Civil War ended. After the war he became superintendent of a southern railroad, before going into life insurance. He died in 1894 at the age of 83 (*Virginia Cavalcade* 1965, 15, no. 2, 43).

As for the *Nashville*, the Secretary of the Navy, Stephen Mallory had no further use for her as a blockade runner. She was therefore handed over to Captain Gooding who represented the ship's new owners, John Fraser and Company of Charleston; they had purchased the ship from the Confederate Government. Her armaments were removed, and before the transfer of ownership all her crew were discharged from the Confederate Navy. After she had safely reached Georgetown, South Carolina, her name was changed to the *Thomas L Wragg* and she became a private blockade runner under the command of Captain Gooding (*ORN*, ser. I, vol. 1, 136-7 and 332; *ORN*, ser. II, vol. 2, 603). A month later the *Nashville/Thomas Wragg* was in at Wilmington, North Carolina, where she landed arms and ammunition and took on a cargo of cotton, before successfully running the blockade on her departure (*ORN*, ser. I, vol. 7, 264-76).

John Fraser and Company then sold the *Thomas Wragg* to a syndicate who planned to use her as a privateer. She was once again re-named this time as the *Rattlesnake*, but on 28 February 1863 she ran aground off Fort McAllister, Georgia, and was subsequently destroyed by the USS *Montauk* under the command of Commander John L. Worden, who

Fig. 18. The CSS *Nashville* running the blockade at Beaufort, North Carolina, in February 1862. Note that the *Nashville* has raised the Union 'Stars and Stripes'.
Harper's Weekly.

had previously commanded John Ericsson's famous USS *Monitor* (*ORN*, ser. II, vol. 1, 261; Denney 1992, 264; Foote 1992, ii, 2).

DISCUSSION

Anglo-American relations were somewhat strained throughout the Civil War by a number of potentially dangerous incidents. The first of these was the '*Trent* Affair' which involved the interception of the Confederate Commissioners Mason and Slidell in November 1861. A second occurring in the same month was the presence in Southampton of the USS *James Adger.* This was almost immediately followed by the incidents described here involving CSS *Nashville*, the *Harvey Birch* and the USS *Tuscarora* (November 1861 to February 1862). *The Times,* for example, stated 'that the battle of the North and South has been transferred from the Potomac to our own waters', and the *Army and Navy Gazette* declared that 'The war was brought close to our own doors. Two navies stand arrayed against one another, at least by deputy, in British waters.' (*The Times* 2.1.1862; *ANG* 11.1.1862.) The events caused even more interest and speculation in the Southampton and Hampshire newspapers, especially in the early months of 1862.

Not surprisingly the Federal Government and the Northern press strongly condemned what appeared to be British sympathy with the presence and actions of the Confederate warship in Southampton. Nevertheless, the British Government attempted through its neutrality laws to keep the two opposing sides apart and prevent an unnecessary confrontation. In the light of the political problems created by the '*Trent* Affair', it is surprising that these Southampton incidents did not push the British Government over the brink. Already in early 1862, the Government began to consider military action against the North. This action included sending a large body of reinforcements to Canada. The sensitivity of the time was also visibly displayed in the Navy's reinforcement of Southampton Water and the Solent in order to ensure the continued separation of the two American warships. The British Government had suddenly found that its traditional role as one of the world's greatest military and naval powers had changed to the role of a neutral power and mediator.

On 9 April 1865, General Robert E. Lee surrendered to General U. S. Grant at Appomattox Court House – the American Civil War was over. Five days later Abraham Lincoln was assassinated in Ford's Theatre, in Washington DC. A bloody chapter in American history was finished, a chapter in which not only North and South had taken part, but also in which Britain had played a role of some importance. However, Hampshire was unique in that it was the only English county which saw 'military action' in the American conflict when both North and South brought their warships to Southampton and the county's coastal waters.

Bibliography

PRIMARY SOURCES
(MANUSCRIPT)
Hampshire Record Office
21M85W/1, diary of Thomas Stopher, 1 January 1862
– 31 December 1863
94M71/PO3, church vestry minutes, Monk
Sherborne
49M69/PV1, church vestry minutes, Hambledon
Photocopy 555/17, church vestry minutes, Wonston

**National Archives and Records Service,
Washington DC**
War Department Records 1861-5, Record and Pension
Office, Record Group 94

Public Record Office
ADM 53, 7900; ADM 53, 8189, Royal Naval ships logs

**Southampton University Library Archives and
Manuscripts**
GC/RU series known as the Palmerston Papers.
Amongst this important collection are the papers
and correspondence of Lord Palmerston during
the time of the Civil War, i.e. 1861-5, sometimes
written from his home at Broadlands, Romsey.
GC/RU/693-9 is of particular interest as
it includes correspondence between Lord
Palmerston and Lord Russell, the Foreign
Secretary, between January and June 1862. The
collection also contains other papers and
correspondence relating to the Civil War.

Virginia Historical Society
MSS1 P 3496C 59-79, the Pegram Papers

PRIMARY SOURCES
(PRINTED)
Army and Navy Gazette
Dictionary of American Naval Fighting Ships 1959-81,
8 volumes, Naval History Division, Office of the
Chief of Naval Operations, Navy Department,
Washington DC
Hampshire Advertiser
*Hampshire Chronicle, Southampton and Isle of Wight
Courier*
Illustrated London News
Navy List, 1862, vol. 2
*Official Records of the Union and Confederate Armies in
the War of Rebellion*, 1889-1901, 128 volumes and
index, US Government Printing Office,
Washington DC (cited as *OR*, series number,
volume number and page number)
*Official Records of the Union and Confederate Navies in
the War of Rebellion*, 1894-1927, 30 volumes and
index, US Government Printing Office,
Washington DC (cited as *ORN*, series number,
volume number and page number)

*Register of Officers of the Confederate States Navy 1861-
1865*, 1931, US Government Printing Office,
Washington DC
*Southampton Times, and Winchester, Portsmouth, Isle of
Wight, and Hampshire Express*
The Times

SECONDARY SOURCES
Adams, E. D. 1925 *Great Britain and the American Civil
War*, vol. 1, New York
Ayling, A. 1895 *Revised Register of New Hampshire
Soldiers and Sailors in the War of Rebellion*, Concord,
New Hampshire
Blume, K. J. 1995 'Coal and Diplomacy in the British
Caribbean during the Civil War' in *Civil War
History* 41
Bourne, K. 1970 *The Foreign Policy of Victorian England*,
Oxford
Crook, D. P. 1974 *The North, the South and the Powers
1861-1865*, New York
Denney, R. E. 1992 *The Civil War Years*, New York
Fairfax, D. McNeill n.d. 'Captain Wilkes' Seizure of
Mason and Slidell' in *Battles and Leaders*, vol. 2,
New Jersey
Ferris, N. D. 1976 *Desperate Diplomacy. William
Seaward's Foreign Policy 1861*, University of
Tennessee
Ferris, N. D. 1977 *The Trent Affair: A Diplomatic Crisis*,
University of Tennessee
Foote, S. 1992 *The Civil War, Fredericksburg to Meridian*
Foote, S. 1992 *The Civil War, Red River to Appomattox*
Hearn, C. G. 1992 *Gray Raiders of the Sea*, Camden,
Maine
Hughes, M. F. 1999 'The Personal Observations of a
Man of Intelligence': Sir James Fergusson's visit
to North America, 1861' in *Civil War History* 45,
no. 2, 240-7
Jones, V. C. 1960 *The Civil War at Sea*, New York
Lonn, E. 1940 *Foreigners in the Confederacy*, University
of North Carolina
Lonn, E. 1951 *Foreigners in the Union Army and Navy*,
Louisiana State University
McPherson, J. M. 1994 *What They Fought For 1861-
1865*, Louisiana State University
Mason, V. (ed.) 1906 *The Public Life and Diplomatic
Correspondence of James Mason*, New York
Musicant, I. 1995 *Divided Waters: the Naval History of
the Civil War*, New York
Nepveux, E. S. 1994 *George Alfred Trenholm and the
Company That Went to War 1861-1865*, Charleston
Patterson, A. T. 1971 *A History of Southampton 1700-
1914, Vol. II The Beginnings of Modern Southampton
1836-1867*, Southampton
Perkins, B. 1993 'The Creation of a Republican Empire
1776-1865' in *The Cambridge History of American
Foreign Relations*, vol. 1, Cambridge

Phisterer, F. 1912 *New York in the War of Rebellion, 1861-1865*, Albany, New York

Robertson, W. M. 1928 *The Confederate Privateers*, Yale University Press

Sifakis, S. 1988 *Who Was Who in the Civil War*, vol. 1, New York

Virginia Cavalcade 1965, 15, no. 2, 38-41, Richmond

Virginia Magazine of History and Biography 1958, 66, 345-50, Richmond

Wise, S. R. 1988 *Lifeline of the Confederacy: Blockade Running During the Civil War*, University of South Carolina

The Civil War shattered the political union of the United States. The Federal Government, however, continued to function, albeit in the hands of a Republican (ie Northern) majority. Federal, therefore, should be understood as shorthand for the North (Unionists). Confederate, on the other hand, refers strictly to the confederation of Southern states which seceded from the Union in 1860-1.

Index
Ship names are given in italics.

Abbreviations

ANG	*Army and Navy Gazette*
DANFS	*Dictionary of American Naval Fighting Ships*
HA	*Hampshire Advertiser*
HC	*Hampshire Chronicle, Southampton and Isle of Wight Courier*
HRO	Hampshire Record Office
ILN	*Illustrated London News*
OR	*Official Records of the Union and Confederate Armies in the War of Rebellion*
ORN	*Official Records of the Union and Confederate Navies in the War of Rebellion*
Pegram	Pegram Papers, Virginia Historical Society
PP	Palmerston Papers, Southampton University Library Archives and Manuscripts
PRO	Public Record Office
ST	*Southampton Times, and Winchester, Portsmouth, Isle of Wight, and Hampshire Express*

Acknowledgements

Note on the author

Firstly, I am indebted to the Virginia Historical Society, Richmond and especially to their Senior Archivist, E. Lee Shephard, for allowing me access to their extensive Civil War library and archives. Secondly I would like to thank Dr John Oldfield of the Department of History at Southampton University who not only encouraged me to produce this Hampshire Paper but who also gave me helpful comments on my draft text. Thirdly I would like to acknowledge the kindness and assistance I have received from the staff of the Southampton University Archives, Hampshire Record Office, the Royal Naval Museum, Portsmouth, Southampton City Archives and the Local History Section of Winchester Library. Finally I owe a debt to my wife Elizabeth without whose support this paper would not have been written.

Michael Hughes was for over 20 years County Archaeologist for Hampshire County Council before he took early retirement in 1996. During his career he produced over 40 academic and professional publications on various aspects of Hampshire's archaeology and landscape history. Since retirement he has been made a Member of Kellogg College, Oxford, and has taken up part-time lecturing for the departments for continuing education at Oxford, Cambridge, Sussex and Southampton universities as well as leading study tours abroad. Having travelled extensively in the eastern United States with his wife, Elizabeth, he has for some years been fascinated by early American history, especially the period of the American Civil War. As a result of this interest he now teaches adult students early American history at Oxford as well as undertaking his own research on English involvement in the Civil War. He has recently had two papers on English aspects of the war published in American Civil War historical journals.